Constitutional Correctness

Trumps

Political Correctness

JOHN SAUER

ISBN 978-1-0980-3037-7 (paperback)
ISBN 978-1-0980-5839-5 (hardcover)
ISBN 978-1-0980-3038-4 (digital)

Christian Faith Publishing, Inc.
832 Park Avenue
Meadville, PA 16335
www.christianfaithpublishing.com

Printed in the United States of America

Prologue

The American Revolution began in 1775 as an open conflict between the thirteen British colonies in America and Great Britain and ended in 1783. The Articles of Confederation was established in 1781 and served as a bridge between the initial government by the Continental Congress of the revolutionary period and the federal government which was established by the US Constitution. The United States Constitution was signed off in 1787. Since 1775, 1,319,943 American lives were lost due to wars. These soldiers died liberating the American colonies from England and establishing the sovereignty of the thirteen colonies, fighting the civil war to establish the essence of the United States and defending the United States against all enemies challenging its sovereignty and threatening its colonies and allies.[1]

> Forty percent of Americans still worked on farms in 1900, but an equal number lived in cities. And by this time, America had surpassed England as the leading industrial nation on earth. The forces responsible for these sweeping transformations were gathering as the 19th century began. The American Revolution broke the back of state-regulated mercantile capitalism and opened the way

---

[1] Militaryfactory.com, 2019

for a market revolution that produced the world's most dynamic economic system.[2]

We call it "political correctness." The name originated as something of a joke, literally in a comic strip, and we tend still to think of it as only half-serious. It is the great disease of our century, the disease that has left tens of millions of people dead in Europe, in Russia, in China—indeed around the world. It is the disease of ideology. Political correctness is not funny. Political correctness is deadly serious.

Political correctness originated in World War I as cultural Marxism and is defined by giving power to the victim class based on race, sex, etc. over the majority.

> A Marxist begins with his prime truth that all evils are sourced in the exploitation of the proletariat by the capitalists. From this he logically proceeds to the revolution to end capitalism, then into the third stage of reorganization into a new social order of the dictatorship of the proletariat, and finally the last stage—the political paradise of communism.[3]

Just as in classical economic Marxism certain groups (i.e. workers and peasants are good, and other groups, i.e., the bourgeoisie and capital owners, are evil). In the cultural Marxism of political correctness, certain groups are good—feminist women (only feminist women, non-feminist women are deemed not to exist), blacks, Hispanics, homosexuals. These groups are determined to be "victims" and therefore automatically good regardless of what any of them do. Similarly, white males are determined automatically to be

---

[2] A Bio. of America: The Rise of Capitalism—Transcript (Miller, 2019)
[3] Alinsky, 2019

evil, thereby becoming the equivalent of the bourgeoisie in economic Marxism.[4]

The Black Book of Communism: Crimes, Terror, Repression, compiled and edited by Stéphane Courtois from the work of several academics, was published in France in 1999 (free download). It is a harrowing account of the crimes of practical communism under regimes such as the USSR, China, Cambodia, North Korea, and those of several African, Latin American, and European countries. It summarizes the death toll as follows:

U.S.S.R.	20 million deaths
China	65 million deaths
Vietnam	1 million deaths
North Korea	2 million deaths
Cambodia	2 million deaths
Eastern Europe	1 million deaths
Latin America	150,000 deaths
Africa	1.7 million deaths
Afghanistan	1.5 million deaths

This adds up to just north of ninety-four million, covering the period 1914 to 1991.

It is important to note that these numbers do not include all deaths, and in particular, do not include deaths due to unsafe drinking water, hunger, or disease. *The Black Book* authors counted only the deaths attributable to crimes by the state against the people, such as deliberate massacres by Communist regimes or formal policies

---

[4]   Academia et al., 2019

that directly led to large-scale deaths such as Maoist China's "great leap forward."[5]

According to a disturbingly pleasant graphic from *Information is Beautiful* entitled simply "20th Century Death," communism was the leading ideological cause of death between 1900 and 2000. The ninety-four million that perished in China, the Soviet Union, North Korea, Afghanistan, and Eastern Europe easily (and tragically) trump the twenty-eight million that died under fascist regimes during the same period.[6]

> In 2017, Professor Stephen Kotkin wrote in The Wall Street Journal that communism killed at least 65 million people between 1917 and 2017: "Though communism has killed huge numbers of people intentionally, even more of its victims have died from starvation as a result of its cruel projects of social engineering."[7]

The Communist Manifesto is an 1848 political pamphlet of Karl Marx and Friedrich Engels' theories concerning the nature of society and politics, that in their own words, "The history of all hitherto existing society is the history of class struggles." It also briefly features their ideas for how the capitalist society of the time would eventually be replaced by socialism. Near the end of the Manifesto, the authors call for "forcible overthrow of all existing social conditions," which served as the justification for all Communist revolutions around the world.[8]

In the United States, over fifty-eight million babies (18 percent of the population) were aborted under the protection of Roe vs Wade Supreme Court ruling handed down in 1973. The percentage of deaths of the American citizens that this court ruling legalized

---

[5] Courtois et al., 1999
[6] Walters, 2013
[7] En.wikipedia.org, 2019
[8] En.wikipedia.org, 2013

greatly exceeds the number of deaths occurring in the expansion of communism in China (approximately .65 percent of China's population) since Mao Zedong led a revolution and the Communist party obtained control in 1947.[9]

The math in the Roe vs Wade and Communist China deaths are for comparative purpose only spanning the lifetime of each ideology. The comparative numbers do not consider the propagation of the populations that did not occur due to the killings.

While addressing Westerners at the embassy on November 18, 1956, in the presence of Polish Communist statesman Władysław Gomułka, First Secretary Khrushchev said: "About the capitalist states, it doesn't depend on you whether or not we exist. If you don't like us, don't accept our invitations, and don't invite us to come to see you. Whether you like it or not, history is on our side. We will bury you!" The speech prompted the envoys from twelve NATO nations and Israel to leave the room.

During Khrushchev's visit to the United States in 1959, the Los Angeles mayor Norris Poulson in his address to Khrushchev stated:

> We do not agree with your widely quoted phrase "We shall bury you." You shall not bury us and we shall not bury you. We are happy with our way of life. We recognize its shortcomings and are always trying to improve it. But if challenged, we shall fight to the death to preserve it.[10]

As nouns, the difference between *progressivism* and *socialism* is that *progressivism* is a political ideology that favors progress towards better conditions in society and ultimately the fulfillment of Karl Marx's communism predictions while *socialism* is the intermediate phase of social development between capitalism and full

---

[9]   Cs.stanford.edu, 2019
[10] En.wikipedia.org, 2019

communism in Marxist theory in which the state has control of the means of production.[11]

As noted above, the US birth rate has been declining slowly over the last several decades. Today, the US fertility rate needed to maintain the current US population is 2.1 children per woman during her lifetime. Yet it now stands at only 1.9 and is falling, so we're going backward.[12]

And speaking of progressives with Communist sympathies, also on *The Nation*'s list is Margaret Sanger. The Planned Parenthood matron visited Stalin's Potemkin villages in 1934. "We could well take example from Russia," Sanger advised Americans upon her return, "where birth control instruction is part of the regular welfare service of the government."

The Planned Parenthood founder was stunned by the explosion in abortions once legalized by the Bolsheviks. No fear, though. Sanger offered this confident prediction: "All the [Bolshevik] officials with whom I discussed the matter stated that as soon as the economic and social plans of Soviet Russia are realized, neither abortions nor contraception will be necessary or desired. A functioning communistic society will assure the happiness of every child, and will assume the full responsibility for its welfare and education."

This was pure progressive utopianism, an absolute faith in central planners.[13]

In 2019, Planned Parenthood is telling American women they are pregnant with a tissue mass and the practitioners will kill the baby as it is being delivered and even after delivery they will set it aside and let it die. This is your baby, and it feels pain. A tissue mass has no heart or brain.

---

[11] WikiDiff, 2019
[12] Investmentoffice.com, 2019
[13] Kangor, 2012

A Strong United States

World War II (often abbreviated to WWII or WW2), also known as the Second World War, was a global war that lasted from 1939 to 1945.

It began September 1, 1939, when Germany invaded Poland, which led Britain and France to declare war on Hitler's Nazi state in retaliation. The primary combatants were the Axis nations of Nazi Germany, Fascist Italy, Imperial Japan, and the Allied nations, Great Britain (and its Commonwealth nations), the Soviet Union, and the United States.[14]

The United States was unwillingly drawn into the war when Japan executed a surprise attack on the US Navy base at Pearl Harbor in Hawaii on December 7, 1941. Japan nearly decimated the US Navy arsenal of eighteen battleships and support ships. The three US aircraft carriers were out to sea on missions ferrying equipment to mainland facilities and were too far away to assist.

The Japanese attack on Pearl Harbor, Hawaii, on December 7, 1941, stunned virtually everyone in the United States military. Japan's carrier-launched bombers found Pearl Harbor totally unprepared. President Franklin Roosevelt quickly addressed Congress to ask for a declaration of war. Congress declared war on Japan on December 8. 1941. Congress declared war on Germany December 11, 1941 just hours after Germany declared war on the United States after the Japanese attack on Pearl Harbor.

---

[14] HistoryNet, 2019

The first American military forces arrived in England on January 26, 1942, a little over a year after the Pearl Harbor attack. The world war ended after Germany unconditionally surrendered to the United States on May 8, 1945, and Japan signed an unconditional surrender document on August 14, 1945.

The United States, a capitalist country, and USSR, a Communist country, are seen as the two world superpowers. The United States overshadows the Union of Soviet Socialist Republics as proven in the subsequent years. The United States is militarily the strongest nation this world has ever seen. The United States is the wealthiest nation this world has ever seen. The United States is the most technologically advanced nation this world has ever seen. The United States is the most benevolent nation this world has ever seen.

Converting Capitalism to Communism

Saul Alynsky was born in Chicago, Illinois on January 30, 1909 to poor Russian Jewish immigrants and died June 12, 1972. Mr. Alynsky was a community organizer and writer. In 1971, he published his book *Rules for Radicals* that laid out thirteen rules to follow on how to successfully run a movement for change. His rules were copied by Democrats and influenced Barack Obama and Hillary Clinton. Professors Richard Cloward and Frances Fox Piven were also students of Saul Alynsky and picked up Saul's community organizing work on his death. They were responsible for the architecture of The National Voter Registration act (Motor Voter Law) that Bill Clinton signed into law in 1993.[15] [16]

Saul Alynsky's Thirteen Rules For Radicals:

1.   *"Power is not only what you have, but what the enemy thinks you have."*

---

[15]   Alinsky, 1971
[16]   Adams, 2014

Power is derived from two main sources—money and people. "Have-nots" must build power from flesh and blood.

In 1968, the Democrat party held their national convention in Chicago. The Vietnam War was underway, and the anti-war left took to the streets to protest the war. The protesters soon turned into rioters and clashed with the Chicago police. The riots turned bloody when the police sought to protect the properties in the area. The media covered the riots as if Students for a Democratic Society (SDS) and other rioters were martyrs of police brutality. This event succeeded in destroying the constitutionally liberal Democrat party, and the Socialists took it over. "Today we are left with a socialist Democrat party steam rolling towards communism."[17]

We are looking to the 2020 elections. Over the last four years, a group referred to as "Black Lives Matter" have been injecting themselves into situations where a black man engaged in criminal activity is killed in the act by a white police officer. Their purpose is to blame law enforcement with the intent of turning the community against law enforcement. Taken to its conclusion, the result would be a lawless community.

Over the last three years another group calling themselves "antifa" have been on the rise.

The *antifa* movement is composed of left-wing, autonomous, militant anti-fascist groups and individuals in the United States. The principal feature of antifa groups is their use of direct action with conflicts occurring both online and in real life. They engage in varied protest tactics, which include digital activism, property damage, physical violence, and harassment against those whom they identify as fascist, racist, or on the far-right.

Activists involved in the movement tend to be anti-capitalists and subscribe to a range of ideologies, typically on the left. They include anarchists, Socialists, and Communists, along with some Liberals and social Democrats. Their stated focus is on fighting far-

---

[17] En.wikipedia.org, 2019

right and white supremacist ideologies directly rather than through electoral means.[18]

Antifa attacks citizens and property causing physical harm intimidating those that are proud of the United States. Their goal appears to be a lawless United States.

2. *"Never go outside the expertise of your people."*

It results in confusion, fear and retreat. Feeling secure ads to the backbone of anyone.

Climate change proponents focus on the political arguments and do not attempt to support their stand with scientific facts. When they are forced into a scientific discussion on climate change, they resort to name calling and personal attacks.[19]

3. *"Whenever possible, go outside the expertise of the enemy."*

Look for ways to increase insecurity, anxiety, and uncertainty.

Rigged polls and false news articles are intended to confuse and distract the Conservatives.

Leading into the 2012 elections, the presidential primaries are fast approaching, and the anxiety is building among the Conservatives trying to decide on their "primary" choice for the Republican nominee for president. Mitt Romney keeps bubbling up as a constant top contender in the polls. Romney's challengers keep changing from week to week, according to the polls. We Conservatives have a "gut" feeling that Romney is not a true Conservative, yet we Conservatives are fearful that our choice of a true Conservative candidate will lose to the current president, according to the polls.

---

[18] En.wikipedia.org, 2019
[19] Climate Change Dispatch, 2017

Let's consider some facts:

The polls are decidedly skewed to benefit the extreme left by choice.

The establishment republicans are noticeably left of center on the political scale.

McCain was the weakest (most moderate) Republican candidate on the 2008 primaries and won the primaries as "the best choice" for the republicans.

McCain lost to the Democratic candidate in the general election.

Mitt Romney is the more notable of the two most Liberal candidates in the 2012 Republican field.

Mitt Romney is consistently one of the top three Republican contenders according to the polls.

The pollsters are ignoring the true Conservative candidates.

The main stream media actively denigrates the Conservative "du jour" in the polls and doesn't touch Romney.

The 2012 election as an example:

Rick Perry rose to the top of the polls instantly and was subsequently denigrated for his immigration stance and his Vagisil executive order. These facts are accurate. He has dropped to the single digits in the polls.

Herman Cain was elevated next in the polls, then sexual abuse charges were levied against him. The accusations originated in the current president's backyard, Chicago, Illinois, in a period 1996 to 1999, when Herman was president and CEO of the National Restaurant Association which is headquartered in Chicago. The accuser could not get other women to back up her charges in the court of public opinion and has disappeared into the woodwork. No such accusations were levied against Herman during his time as president of Godfather's Pizza where he successfully brought the company out of bankruptcy nor his time with Burger King where he returned a segment of Detroit Burger King franchises out of near bankruptcy to among the most profitable Burger Kings in the country. Herman has dropped back in the polls but still remains in the top three.

The next candidate to be elevated into the sunlight of the polls is Newt Gingrich. Under examination, he is found to be liberal in his approach to the "illegal immigrants" issue. He wants to make the residing illegal immigrants legal occupants in the United States while closing the border to further illegals. The only way I see this being acceptable is if they are denied the voting rights that American citizens have.

I expect that if the main stream media can find something with which to denigrate Michelle Bachmann and Rick Santorum, they will bubble to the top of the polls for scrutiny against Romney.

Mitt Romney has not received the proctology examination which has been given to the top Conservative candidates. Mitt is the 2012 John McCain. The nation's bane, The Affordable Care Act, AKA "Obamacare," is modeled after Massachusetts's near-bankrupt state healthcare system which Romney shoehorned in when he was governor of Massachusetts. Mitt is also a proponent of the scientifically debunked and ethically defamed global warming movement. These are two of the main platforms of progressive POTUS 44. Romney will be easy pickings for the progressives in 2012 if he is the chosen Republican candidate. Romney became the elected Republican candidate for president. He lost handily.

The electorate finally got it right in the 2016 Presidential election for POTUS 45.

4. *"Make the enemy live up to its own book of rules."*

If the rule is that every letter gets a reply, send thirty thousand letters. You can kill them with this because no one can possibly obey all of their own rules.

The left has used this so many times over the past decades, and the right has no counter for it because the left has no rules they have set for themselves. Turning the other cheek doesn't cut it, it just gives the Socialists fresh meat to slap around.

Today the socialist sponsors are overwhelming the southern border of the United States by sponsoring immigrant caravans consisting of thousands of immigrants through Mexico to the southern

US border. If they cross the border, they become criminals in our country and should be deported to the last man, woman, and child.

5. *"Ridicule is man's most potent weapon."*

There is no defense. It's irrational. It's infuriating. It also works as a key pressure point to force the enemy into concessions.

The socialist Democrats have worn out every negative pronoun and adjective they have trying to label POTUS 45. Every accusation they threw at him proved to be a lie. We know their game now, and it would be laughable if they did not cost the taxpayers so much money.

6. *"A good tactic is one your people enjoy."*

They'll keep doing it without urging and come back to do more. They're doing their thing and will even suggest better ones.

It seems the only things left they enjoy are bashing Christians, police, and Conservatives.

7. *"A tactic that drags on too long becomes a drag."*

Don't become old news.

We noted this in the first two and a half years of POTUS 45. After six months of attacks by the Socialists, it was obvious that they could not make their allegations against Trump stick, but they were determined to keep trying even though their base was slowly leaving them.

8. *"Keep the pressure on. Never let up."*

Keep trying new things to keep the opposition off balance. As the opposition masters one approach, hit them from the flank with a new one.

The socialist Democrats have gone so far as to attack the wife and children of their target.

This was in play against POTUS 45 for two and a half years. Every accusation of criminality was proven to be a lie.

9. *"The threat is usually more terrifying than the thing itself."*

Imagination and ego can dream up many more consequences than any activist.

The Socialists said President Trump will start World War III when he announced his intentions to put sanctions on North Korea, China, and Mexico to pressure them to do the right thing. Mexico began enforcing their own laws, and the immigrant invasion on our southern border dropped to a trickle. There are still thousands of "immigrants" that need to be vetted.

North Korea and China are holding out hoping President Trump is defeated in 2020.

10. *"The major premise for tactics is the development of operations that will maintain a constant pressure upon the opposition."*

It is this unceasing pressure that results in the reactions from the opposition that are essential for the success of the campaign.

11. *"If you push a negative hard enough, it will push through and become a positive."*

Violence from the other side can win the public to your side because the public sympathizes with the underdog.

In 1969, the civil riots and general uprisings around the Democratic convention in Chicago, Illinois made way for the Communist takeover of the Democrat party. The media aided the rioters by describing them as victims of the police.

Today antifa and other less organized groups are employing similar tactics. They destroy civil order by challenging civil laws thus goading the police into action then claiming police brutality.

12. *"The price of a successful attack is a constructive alternative."*

Never let the enemy score points because you're caught without a solution to the problem.

The crisis at the southern border is caused by the Socialist sympathizers. They are organizing the caravans and sustaining them on their march north to the United States border. Their solution is to leave the border open. This solves nothing and is unacceptable.

13. *"Pick the target, freeze it, personalize it, and polarize it."*

Cut off the support network and isolate the target from sympathy. Go after people and not institutions; people hurt faster than institutions.

This rule is employed in the first two years of POTUS 45's first term. There were numerous attempts at discouraging the Conservatives from supporting their elected president. We weren't discouraged. It appears the socialist Democrat party, the mainstream media, and the establishment have lost their credibility with the American voters. Life is getting better.

AINO

It is getting difficult to distinguish between progressives, liberals, and RINOs. They all seem to be working toward the same goal—the destruction of the American way of life and the capitalist system. Instead of getting bogged down trying to figure the correct label to apply to any such elected official, I have settled on an acronym for a new label that groups them: *AINO (American In Name Only)*.

Pinning Down the Meaning of Extremist

We hear the terms "extremists," "right wingers," and the like frequently from the left without a definition of the words. That leaves it up to each individual to supply his own meaning for the term. When said with a sneer, it surely means something negative, doesn't it? The technique was successfully employed in a 2008 campaign, "Hope & Change." Instead of a sneer, it was pitched with a smile. The definition of the term was left to each listener. You heard comments such as: "Halleluiah, I don't have to pay my mortgage anymore," "I am going to have my kitchen repaired, finally." Nobody thought to ask the author what he meant by "Hope & Change."

So we are on the same page, let's understand the term *extreme* and give *extremist* an anchor point. The term *extreme* implies a linear relationship of two anchor points. From one end of the line, the other end is the extreme distance away. In today's political lexicon, the two points are referred to as the left and the right. The definitions are left up to each individual in the audience. In order to understand each other, we need to agree on the definitions of the terms in context.

On your extreme right, you have the Constitution of the United States. Under the guidelines of this constitution, a capitalist society has evolved and the United States became the shining light on the top of the hill. The United States has the mightiest military the world has ever seen, the country has the richest citizens the world has ever seen, the citizens are the most technically advanced the world has ever seen, and the United States is the most benevolent country this world has ever seen. Those whose ideals stand in close proximity to the constitution are the "extreme right."

On your extreme left, you have Communists, Socialists, kings, and dictators. I see socialism as "dictatorship and majestic rule by committee," as defined under Politburo. The major goal of those on the left is to snuff out the shining light on the hill because it gives their subjects *hope*. To this end, those on the left name call those on the right: extremists, right wingers, radical right, etc. They don't refer to those on the right as constitutionalists or constitutional conservatives. Adding these two terms to the volley of names for those on the right would show the uninformed that the left is against the constitution of the United States and everything it represents.

When you hear someone lobbing the "extreme" term in a discussion about politics, ask him if he is referring to the extreme left or extreme right. If he answers the right, take a stand and tell them, "That is the constitutional right."

In the United States, constitutional correctness trumps political correctness wherever the two are in conflict.

Am I a Radical?

Have you ever been called a radical or you have radical views? I have. Between elections I have had time to ask myself, "Am I a radical?" The left has corrupted so many common words that I decided I had better consult the dictionary to get a fresh start toward my understanding of the meaning of *radical*. I find that there is no such thing as a "radical" right unless it is in defense of the constitution. Those of us who believe in the Constitution of the United States are on the right. Those of us that absolutely believe in the constitution are on the far right. The degree of difference between the two depends on how liberal the person is when understanding the intent of the Constitution.

A radical by definition advocates extreme measures to retain or restore a political state of affairs, the *radical* right. Another important element in the definition of radical is having extreme political or social views that are not shared by most people and is associated with political views, practices, and policies of extreme change. We choose to retain the constitutional status of the United States and not change it. The left chooses to change the constitution showing disdain for the founding fathers ideals that made the United States of America the great nation that it is.

An example of radical activity is displayed by Students for a Democratic Society and the Black Panthers in 1969 attacking the Chicago police to turn the public against law enforcement. Black Lives Matter and antifa in the mid-2010s with the same goal in mind on the national level.

Am I a Terrorist?

I'm trying to understand how Conservative American citizens can be referred to as terrorists by the 25 percent of progressive Americans and AINOs. I am a radical Conservative. Other American Conservatives don't terrify me. You don't terrify me. Do I terrify you?

Merriam Webster defines terrorism: "the use of violent acts to frighten the people in an area as a way of trying to achieve a political goal."

The Tea Party is most referred to as an example of a homegrown terrorist group. So are military veterans, gun owners, and anyone who swore an oath to or simply supports the Constitution of the United States. I examine the Tea Party's behavior under the sun. They are known to wave signs on street corners to publicize an issue that might not be reported in the mainstream media or is under reported in the media. That does not terrify me. Does it terrify you?

Tea Party members are known to attend public meetings and ask questions pertinent to the legislation being considered at that meeting. It is their right as taxpayers to understand the legislation before it is implemented. That doesn't terrify me. Does it terrify you? It might terrify the legislators who are asked for an accounting of the legislation.

Tea Party members and other Conservative groups convened in Washington, DC to express their disapproval of several issues including Obamacare. That does not terrify me. Does it terrify you? It might terrify the legislators who appear to forget their campaign promises and ignore their voters and taxpayers.

Tea Party members and other Conservative groups refuse to give up their Second Amendment right to bear arms. This wasn't amended to the constitution to give gun owners a right to hunt for food and sport. They already have that right. This amendment gives American citizens the right to protect themselves from a tyrannical government. That does not terrify me. Does it terrify you? It might terrify the legislators who ignore their country's constitution and allow dictatorial powers to an extremely radical president who ignores the constitution and the elected Conservative lawmakers.

The Tea Party terrifies the elected legislators that forget or ignore the promises they made to get elected. The Tea Party does not terrorize the American citizens. Some of the citizens may fear the Tea Party because they get all their information from the mainstream media. Those numbers are dwindling as seen in the ratings for the alphabet news channels.

I am a Conservative radical and am pleased to terrify the rogue politicians and POTUS 44.

Am I Being Anal?

I need to vent, and I choose you as my sounding board. I have had discussions with candidates, campaign workers, and people I associate closely with about my assessments. I explain my position on the candidates' views in the following way.

I look for *specificity*—the aftermath of "Hope & Change" has made me highly sensitive to candidates that use broad brushstrokes to paint their picture to the public. One candidate states when speaking about non-life-threatening aid to illegals starts out, "In general I am opposed to" and finishes up with "the money should go back where it belongs, to the people." Illegal immigrants are people too. I look for the money going back to the citizen taxpayers. I don't assume the politician's definition mirrors my hopes for his response. These politicians will be writing our legislation when elected. Remember "Affordable Care Act"?

I will be termed anal for my "tight anal" views, but I refuse to assume the position that gave us POTUS 44 in 2008.

To Compromise or Not

The Progressives have successfully convoluted so much of our English language, I feel a need to start by going back to the dictionary again to reread the definition of *compromise*:

Main Entry: ¹*com·pro·mise*
Pronunciation: käm-pr-mz
Function: *noun*

1. a settlement of a dispute by each party giving up some demands
2. a giving up to something that is wrong or degrading: *surrender* <a *compromise* of one's principles>
3. the thing agreed upon as a result of a compromise

The parties involved in the debt limit compromise are Democrats, Republicans, and Conservatives.

As I see it, a compromise leads to a successful end when the parties involved have the same goal but chose different paths to achieve that goal. They may have to compromise on some points to reach the goal. The result is satisfactory to all involved.

A compromise involving parties that have different goals is illogical and results in a confused and unsatisfactory end to all parties.

The Democrats' goal is to grow government, and to continue toward this goal, they need the debt ceiling lifted. The Republicans' goal is to get along with the Democrats and placate the upstart Conservatives among the Republicans by reducing government spending. The Conservatives' goal is to reduce spending, shrink government, and lower the debt ceiling.

The "compromise" between the Democrats and Republicans is to raise the debt ceiling, reduce future government spending increases, and no reduction in government programs. The Conservative taxpayer goals are not represented.

The Democrats pulled the Republicans by the nose ring, further left. There aren't enough Conservatives in Congress to overcome the "old guard" and RINO Republicans.

Compromise has no logical application in this disagreement. This was a political war of differing ideologies that needed to be fought to the end. It may have resulted in a political standoff until the 2016 elections are finalized, but the ultimate end would have been clearly defined. In the meantime, POTUS 44 would have to revert to dictator and raise the debt ceiling by executive order.

The State of the Union

An Immigrant's Perspective

I immigrated in 1949 as a child with my siblings and mother and father after a three-year wait for someone to pay for passage for a family of seven. We were displaced from our farm in Yugoslavia during the Second World War, and our home was taken over by the invaders.

Our family received passage to the United States in 1949. I was naturalized nine years later when my parents earned their citizenship. In those nine years, my father and brother purchased a home, paid it off, doubled its square footage, and put a basement under it.

While I was growing up, the United States was designing and building improved computers. My nephews were able to buy an American-made Commodore 64 computer for the home and soon replace it with a Tandy computer and so on.

The United States began its space program and quickly progressed to manned space flights and building a space station in cooperation with several countries including Canada, Russia, and Japan. The US reusable space shuttles were the workhorses for this cooperative effort.

The apex of United States worldwide influential domination was reached in the mid-sixties. The American citizens became complacent in their security and worldwide influence. Their tolerance of political changes and the progressive movement allowed anti-American organization such as Students for a Democratic Society (SDS) and the Black Panthers to rise up and disrupt American society. Many of the principals and leaders of these groups were tried and jailed, but the undoing of the American society had been carried forward by those leaders who planned and funded these groups.

A major reversal in the American education system occurred with the launching of the United States Department of Education in the early '70s. At that time the United States was ranked third in the world for its education system. The state that was ranked fiftieth in the United States was still within the boundaries of the country that was ranked third in the world. Since the inception of the Department of Education, the United States has dropped to twenty-seventh in the world in education all the while insisting that no child is left behind. The American citizens didn't notice that the entire country was falling behind the rest of the world.

The United States entered WWII bloodied and greatly weakened by a sneak attack at Pearl Harbor on December 7, 1941. When WWII ended on V-day in 1945, the United States was recognized as a victor and a world military power. It was obvious that isolationism was not the way to peace for the United States. Total military and civilian casualties of WWII are estimated at fifty-five to eighty million citizens of the countries involved in the war.

Then came the Korean War. United States General MacArthur had destroyed the Korean army and was on his way into China when the DC politicians stopped him and agreed with China to split the North and South of Korea at the thirty-eighth parallel. There were an estimated five million casualties. There is still no peace in the Koreas.

The Vietnam War was fought on two fronts, by the US military against Viet Cong and by the anti-war (anti-American) media in the United States against the US citizens public opinion. The media reported the daily count of American casualties and the location of the military encounters. The media kept getting louder as the war progressed and the politicians finally decided to call it quits. Again the military planning was overturned by the politicians who gave up and quit the war. The casualties are estimated at 3.3 million enemy combatants and civilians and 58 thousand US military. Years later, a Viet Cong general admitted that they were within days of surrendering to the United States.

The Iraq wars saw the introduction of smart bombs and lethal drones and the use of Special Forces and collaborators to collect the intelligence that enabled the precision targeting for these spectacular weapons. This combination greatly reduced the military and civilian casualty rate. There were approximately five-hundred thousand deaths in this war over an eight-year period. With the new successes of these precision weapons, the commander-in-chief POTUS 44 gave the military leaders new "suicidal" rules of engagement which increased military deaths which in turn gave the media more red meat to throw at the military effort. Still, the body count wasn't enough to raise public outcry against continued military involvement in Iraq.

The precision weapons proved to reduce both the military and civilian deaths. These precision weapons require accurate ground intelligence to pinpoint the targets. Without accurate intelligence, these smart weapons are no more that spitballs on the blackboard. Who will cooperate with the American intelligence agencies knowing that they may very well be marked for death for aiding the United States military because the American media publicizes not just the victories but detail behind the victories?

The anti-American media published American secrets that were protected by responsible journalist in the prior century, up to and through WWII. They publicized excerpts from military manuals as torture techniques, published photos from Abu Ghurayb Prison to shame the military in Iraq, all to the detriment of the successful military effort in Iraq. They published how intelligence was being collected in the war zones exposing the sources to lethal retribution by the enemy.

If the smart weapons are neutralized, the United States will have to revert back to carpet bombing to stop an enemy. The anti-American media will then have plenty of red meat again to continue demeaning the United States in the eyes of the world.

The mainstream media is as much an enemy of the United States and its constitution as is communism and radical Islam.

Today, computers are built and improved in foreign countries. Our continuing success in space is dependent on the cooperation of an enemy country which is getting more hostile toward the United States. Since the US Department of Education's inception, the US students' education ranking among the world's students dropped from third to twenty-seventh, and the mainstream media is behind the weakening and demoralization of the what is the world's mightiest military. But we accept political correctness, tolerate all beliefs, and open our arms to all who want to enter these United States. No other country in the world is as accepting and tolerant as the United States, and it is costing the United States dearly.

As for myself, I will oppose the current trend until I die. I find no pride in leaving a political and social wasteland to my grandchildren. This is not what my father had in mind when he brought his family to the United States from a Communist country.

Education

History

The federal government's first Department of Education (ED) was created in 1867—based on legislation signed into law by President Andrew Johnson—as a non-cabinet-level agency charged with collecting information on schools and teaching to help states establish effective school systems. By the following year, the Department of Education was reduced to a minor office, ultimately buried inside the Department of the Interior. It was operated by four employees on a budget of $15,000.

With the passage of the Second Morrill Act in 1890, this small bureau was given the responsibility for administering support for the original system of land-grant colleges and universities. In 1939, it was moved out of the Department of the Interior and placed in the newly established Federal Security Agency (FSA), where its name was changed to the Office of Education.

During the World War I and World War II eras, federal education officials became responsible for providing federal aid to vocational education. The 1917 Smith-Hughes Act and the 1946 George-Barden Act focused on agricultural, industrial, and home economics training for high school students. The Lanham Act in 1941 and the Impact Aid laws of 1950 eased the burden on communities affected by the presence of military and other federal installations by making payments to school districts.

In 1953, the Eisenhower administration abolished the FSA and transferred most of its functions to a newly created cabinet-level agency, the Department of Health, Education, and Welfare (HEW). The 1950s also saw federal lawmakers adopt the National Defense Education Act (NDEA) in 1958 in response to the Soviet launch of Sputnik. To help ensure that highly trained individuals would be available to help America compete with the Soviet Union in scientific and technical fields, the NDEA included support for loans to college students, the improvement of science, mathematics, and foreign language instruction in elementary and secondary schools, graduate fellowships, foreign language and area studies, and vocational-technical training.

In 1979, the Carter administration decided that education was too important for it to be part of HEW and established the cabinet-level ED to bolster its mission of supporting schools and educational systems around the country at the state and local level.

Reagan promised during the 1980 presidential election to eliminate the department as a cabinet post, but Democrats in the House refused to go along. Bennett was an outspoken critic of the educational establishment, which he called "the blob" for bloated educational bureaucracy. He advocated for teacher testing, performance-based pay, education accountability, ending tenure, a national exam for all students to take, and school vouchers to allow parents to send their children to private schools.[20]

Each of the fifty states was responsible for the management of their education systems and management. In 1974, the Federal Department of Education decided it was unfair that a state should be ranked the fiftieth state in education in the United States and usurped the creation of the standards from the states and created standards that all fifty states must meet.

---

[20] Allgov.com, 2019

I was present at a meeting on August 8, 2013 where the speaker was from FloridaPromise.org. She spoke on the benefits of the Common Core Curriculum. There were many questions from the floor, and the floor chairman didn't have time to get to all the questions, including mine. So I emailed my question:

"Your timeline for pointing out the weaknesses that Common Core will correct in our education system starts in 1999. My experience in the American education system starts in 1951 when I entered first grade and goes on into the '60s. During that time, America's education system ranked second or third in the world for quality and production, and Mississippi was ranked last of the fifty United States in education. Each state was totally responsible for the funding, education, and testing of their students through their local school boards. In the mid-sixties, the socialist groups like Students for a Democratic Society and Black Panthers shook up the status quo through civil insurrection. In the late sixties, some politicians took the opportunity to point to Mississippi and say, "What a shame there is so much disparity in education between the states" and succeeded in establishing the Federal Department of Education in Washington, DC. At that time the US education still ranked second or third in the world.

"The Department of Education started usurping the states' education responsibilities by setting education standards that all states must target. These standards kept evolving through the years as new education experiments were tried. A few years after each new federal education experiment was implemented, the US education ranking in the world dropped one or two points. I see that the United States ranks seventeenth in the world today.

"I finally get to the question: Have Common Core standards been evaluated against the educational standards of the fourteen countries that have surpassed the United States while the US Department of Education has been "updating education standards" in the US?"

Her reply stated that the education standards of fifty years ago do not serve our children today and promised an answer to my question soon.

I replied:

"The education standards of fifty years ago and beyond gave us the talent that got us into space, engineered and miniaturized the computer, and made the United States the world leader in innovation. Now, our space program is dependent on launches from foreign countries launch pads, the further miniaturization of computers are being accomplished in foreign countries, and innovation is being strangled by federal regulations. We are told this is the new norm, get used to it.

"The updated education standards dismiss the importance of sports and arts, the pride of mastering cursive handwriting, and the benefit of performing basic calculations without the aid of a digital pad in hand. We are a very long way from designing artificial intelligence that can innovate. To innovate, our students must have a wide range of experiences and abilities to be able to imagine an innovation.

"Common Core Standards will be narrowing the students' education even further. The curriculum's narrowing the breath of the students' education in order to increase the depth seems to be a movement to channel the students' education into a narrowing choice of fields of employment available to the students.

"Until fifty years ago, I understood that elementary education gave the students a working knowledge of the three Rs—Reading, (W)riting, and (A)rithmatic. High school gave the students an introduction to the major areas of advanced education. Upon graduation from high school, the students could choose to go exceedingly deeper into their chosen disciplines through the university system. The student could choose to enroll into a community college such as Indiana Vocational Technical School or Florida Community College. The student could choose to enter the work force with a high school education and return to higher education when his goals change.

"I don't understand how narrowing the students' choices benefits the students and the United States. I am curious to learn what the fourteen countries that surpassed us in education in the last fifty years have done differently to update their education system for the future. It is obvious that the United States education standards are no longer a model for the world."

I never received the response promised.

A major reversal in the American education system occurred with the launching of the United States Department of Education in the early '70s. At that time, the United States was ranked third in the world for its education system. The state that was ranked fiftieth in the United States was still within the boundaries of the country that was ranked third in the world. Since the inception of the Department of Education, the United States has dropped to twenty-seventh in the world in education all the while insisting that no child is left behind. The American citizens didn't notice that the entire country was falling behind.

The US Department of Education has failed to deliver the promises made in establishing the cabinet level post. It is destroying the American education system while transforming it into a socialist indoctrination system. A logical move to reverse the degradation of American education is to return control of education to each state as was the structure that "made America great."

With political correctness, common knowledge and common sense began being twisted around 180 degrees from the norm. This has been accomplished by the federal government usurping educational system from the states. Until the 1970s, each state was responsible for their education system. The teachers unions had to negotiate forty-eight contracts, one with each state. New York rated the highest test scores, and Mississippi rated the lowest. In the 1960s, the government federalized the education system to standardize the curriculum and educational test results thus eliminating the discrepancies in test results across the nation. The results under the state-controlled education system were unfair to the children in Mississippi. Then came court ordered busing because some neighborhood schools were still producing better test results than their neighbors. This didn't produce the desired results so the curriculum was dumbed down, and the extra-curricular activities were dropped so the teachers and administrators could continue getting their raises in spite of the poor performance of the students. This was all made possible when the nation's education system was consolidated under one teaching contract.

CONSTITUTIONAL CORRECTNESS TRUMPS
POLITICAL CORRECTNESS

The products of the American education system predating the federalization of education were responsible for defeating communism and socialism, winning two world wars and allowing millions of Europeans to embrace democracy. They were responsible for developing and deploying the atomic bomb which ended the Second World War sooner and saving tens of thousands more American lives in fighting a nation that, taking advantage of Hitler's war in Europe, was hell bent on domination of the rest of the world. They were responsible for developing the technology needed to land Americans on the moon, explore Mars, and miniaturize computers so they can be embedded unobtrusively in most of our daily lives.

The educational revolution of the '70s included a wave of Marxists and Maoists in our colleges and universities. A good friend of mine carried the little red book around campus. It was the cool thing to do. I wasn't cool. They are the leaders of today, the decision-makers for our future.

The products of the resulting education system are journalist that espouse anti-capitalism and anti-militarism. We now have educators that are openly anti-American, anti-capitalist. The Vietnam War was lost because the journalists wanted it so. Not because the journalists were against the war but because the journalists did not want America to succeed.

Today, the products of the resulting education system have elected a president that runs around apologizing to the Muslim world for the past victories of America.

For the last twenty years, we have been amazed at the stupidity of ideas that the Democrat leaders have been espousing and legislating. They are the product of our education system. They were educated at Princeton, Oxford, Yale, and other elite universities. They are not stupid. As I noted earlier, the American education system has been degraded from being second or third in the world to rating twenty-seventh in the world. They feel we Americans have been dumbed down enough to believe whatever they say.

Why the Progressive Movement Can't Grow Followers

Approaching the 2010 general elections, Obama's popularity is reaching new bottoms, and his supporters are abandoning him. He will not fall below 30-percent popularity because of the elitists and their influence over the nonchalant voters they influence.

My reasoning is that the progressives dominate the education system and have degraded the educational curriculum to make the lowest achiever set the standard of measurement for scholastic achievement. Those capable of higher achievement are bored and turn their attention to other diversions such as drugs and social networks. I'm not saying drugs and social networks are interchangeable or lead into each other. For the general population of young voters, the drugs and social networks fill the void left in the wake of the progressive movement. The movement has disenfranchised the very voters it groomed to follow it.

With this limitation, the progressives have created on their movement by losing the youth they groomed in the government schools the only way I see them achieving their goal is through force. Obama has expressed a desire to create a domestic military force that will rival our standing army. He and preceding Democrat presidents have made cuts in our national military forces. This degrades our national security making us more vulnerable to attack and more dependent on external support such as the United Nations. The president's control over the population grows with the activation of the domestic military force. The roots of this domestic military could be the "new Black Panther party" that tested the waters in Philadelphia during the 2008 elections. They were dressed in military style uniforms and acting in a threatening manner at the polls. Obama's government saw nothing wrong with this because Eric Holder, Obama's choice for attorney general, stopped the trial just before it was turned over to a jury. The general population and attorneys in the AG's office saw this as a cut and dry case of voter intimidation.

Back to the disenfranchised voters.

This country has a large population of youth floating in a sea of drugs and social networks void of social and ethical constraints.

They need to be educated in the three pillars that made the United States great—the constitution, capitalism, and the role religion has in the American society. The progressive government won't do that. The government schools stopped teaching these basics since they usurped the control of education from the states back in the early '60s using Mississippi as an example of the disparate results in education among the fifty states ("Mississippi was ranked last in the "national test scores"). In these fifty years, there is still disparity in the test scores even though the government test standards have been dropped to where we can't point to Mississippi as having the weakest education system. The disparity now exists between private and parochial schools and the government schools with the federal education system replacing Mississippi as the example of why the national education system needs to be overhauled. The control of education needs to be returned to the states and a voucher system can be implemented to allow out of state student to attend school in higher-rated states or parochial and private education institutions. Concurrently, the State Board of Education and the state teachers union can put their heads together to improve their system and provide reasons for the students to be happy with the state education.

Until the public education system returns to teaching the basics instead of indoctrinating the youth, I propose a grassroots curriculum teaching the United States Constitution, the basics of capitalism, the role of religion in a free society and patriotic American history. This approach will restore American pride that has been eroded in the last fifty years. It will give the achievers a foundation to build on and a sense of purpose.

2011 Land of Oz

Who has not seen the movie *The Wonderful Wizard of Oz*? It was first published in 1901 by the George M. Hill Company in Chicago. Briefly, it follows the adventures of four characters, a scarecrow who is looking for a brain, a lion whose is looking for courage, and a tin man who is looking for a heart. Dorothy is looking for the wizard who will help her get back to the comfort and security of her home in Kansas. The book was written by L. Frank Baum as a children's book.

This story is playing out in today's political world. The three attributes sorely lacking in Dorothy's world are missing from the executive, legislative and judicial branches of government. The judicial branch lacks the wisdom to understand the Constitution of the United States. The legislative branch lacks the courage to honor the Constitution of the United States in the face of a rogue executive branch that has no heart for the citizens of the United States.

The citizens AKA taxpayers, AKA voters, AKA Tea Party are trying to find their way back to the safety and security of their home in the Democratic republic of the United States. After Dorothy, in her anger, pushed aside the curtain to talk to and understand the wizard, the scarecrow found his brain, the lion found his courage, and the tin man found his heart. Dorothy had been in awe of the wizard and found her way back home to Kansas after she finally pushed aside the curtain and saw and spoke to the man that was hiding behind it.

The transition from the scarecrow, the lion, and the tin man to the three branches of government may be weak, and you can punch holes in the similes, but you then miss the point. Each and every one of you voters is Dorothy.

The American voter has been conditioned to have great expectations of the candidate that has the most money in his war chest *"because this is the man who will win the election."* The American voter's wizard is hidden by a curtain of money. Until the voter gets angry enough to push aside the curtain and understand the man, he will be paralyzed by the awesome curtain and will remain lost in the world of the wizard.

My Analysis of the 2008 Primaries

Like most people, I haven't been paying much attention to primary elections for most of my life. The primaries have historically had very low turnout, about 15 percent.

The 2008 primaries were no different for me. However, timing of the primaries was changed from the usual May/June time frame for some select states to a distributed schedule spanning January to April. I didn't pay much attention to the change. Florida and Michigan Republican parties were penalized for moving their primaries too far ahead of the proposed schedule limits. The Republicans had a half dozen candidates in the primaries, most of whom were Conservative. McCain was the most liberal of them. I liked Huckabee's inclusion of the fair tax in his agenda but was disappointed in his stand against the death penalty. That left me favoring Thompson and Romney. But this was only the primaries, and I remained cool toward the process. I was psyched up for the main event in November.

The early primaries were held in liberal states, and the DNC declared early on that McCain was their choice for the Republican presidential nominee. I thought, *Thanks, but we will choose our own.*

McCain went on to take an early lead over the Conservative candidates. By the time the Conservative states primaries were scheduled my two republican choices dropped out, others fell away in short order. McCain had too much of a lead. Huckabee was the only one that stayed in the primary to the end with McCain.

McCain lost handily in the main event. How could a seasoned politician lose to a political newbie?

How can this happen?

The way I see it: The early primaries were held in liberal states and Hillary led Obama early in the Democratic primary. Neither DNC candidate was viable against a conservative Republican. The DNC gambled and had their voters cross party lines to help elect the weakest Republican in the field. Democrat voters were either going to vote for the Democrat of their choice in the primary and lose the general election to a strong Republican, or they could vote as Republican for the primary and vote for McCain as the DNC's choice for the Republican candidate. They could vote for their Democrat candidate in the general election. Party affiliation does not restrict your vote choice in the general election. Hillary assumed she would have the primary won by May and had no campaign strategy after April. With McCain well on his way to giving the Democrats a winnable election and Hillary out of gas, the radicals in the DNC could concentrate their minions on electing the most radical candidate we have ever seen. In May, Obama's campaign picked up steam, and he won the Democratic nomination for president. McCain won the Republican primary.

With the general election pitting a RINO (Republican In Name Only) against the Democratic candidate, the Conservatives saw no desirable choice and stayed home once again as they did in the primaries. Obama was elected POTUS 44.

The Democrats won the 2008 presidential election in the primaries. With a 15-percent Conservative voter turnout for the primaries it doesn't take many acorns to swing the Republican primary election to the weakest candidate. If you continue to sit out the primary elections, you will not change a thing and the Socialists will continue dictating to you how Americans will live and behave.

Unions, Lobbyists, Patriots, Oh My!
Putting This in Perspective

The unions spend a lot of money endorsing the candidate that they expect and demand will favor unions at the negotiation table. At negotiations with the politicians is when they collect on the endorsement money they put out at the elections. The unions collect dues every payday from the union members. The more members they have, the more money they collect and the more money they have to endorse favorable candidates when elections come around. Public sector unions collect dues from government workers. Government workers are paid from money taken from taxpayers in the form of taxes, fees, and fines.

When a public sector union contract approaches the end of its contractual lifespan, the union leaders and politicians enter negotiations to create the terms for the next contract period. The two sides haggle with taxpayer money and almost always results in an increase in taxes. The taxpayers who pay the bill are not involved in the negotiations.

The lobbyists are paid representatives of private companies or organizations who seek to bring about the passage or defeat of legislative bills or to influence their content in favor or benefit of the private companies or organizations. Example: legislation can favor the commercial citrus growers when it declares homeowners are not allowed to plant citrus trees within ten feet of a home foundation; legislation can favor a business sector if it declares a government contract worth more than $500,000 must be awarded to a company with no less than fifty employees even if a smaller company can do the job for less money. The homeowners with zero lot lines have to purchase their citrus commercially, and the high-dollar government contracts are awarded to higher cost companies at a higher cost to the taxpayers.

Tea Party patriots are taxpayers and voters who want their government to represent those who elected them to office. The politicians are entrusted with our money and the future of the city and country we reside in. We want the most Conservative politicians we can find to be these stewards. The unions are organized and so are the lobbyists. Organized taxpayers are a threat to both of them. With the Tea Party organization, we are sheep to be shorn no more.

Although the tea party is not visible on the corners as in the past, the movement exists in each of us Conservative voters.

Steering Conservatives to the Weakest Candidate

The presidential primaries are fast approaching, and the anxiety is building among the Conservatives trying to decide on their "primary" choice for the Republican nominee for president. Mitt Romney keeps bubbling up as a constant top contender in the polls. Romney's challengers keep changing from week to week, according to the polls. We Conservatives have a "gut" feeling that Romney is not a true Conservative yet we Conservatives are fearful that our choice of a true Conservative candidate will lose to POTUS 44, according to the polls.

Let's consider some facts:
The polls are decidedly skewed to benefit the extreme left by intent.

The establishment Republicans are noticeably left of center on the political scale.

The Democrats declared McCain as the best candidate of the Republican field.

McCain was the weakest (most moderate) Republican candidate on the 2008 primaries and won the primaries as

"the best choice for the Republicans."

McCain lost to Obama in the general election.

Mitt Romney is the more notable of the two most liberal candidates in the 2012 Republican field.

Mitt Romney is consistently one of the top three Republican contenders according to the polls.

The establishment Republicans are ignoring the true Conservative candidates.

The mainstream media actively denigrates the conservative "du jour" in the polls and doesn't touch Romney.

Rick Perry rose to the top of the polls instantly and was subsequently denigrated for his immigration stance and his Vagisil executive order. These facts are accurate. He has dropped to the single digits in the polls.

Herman Cain was elevated next in the polls, then sexual abuse charges were levied against him. The accusations originated in Obama's backyard, Chicago, Illinois in a period, 1996 to 1999, when Herman was president and CEO of the National Restaurant Association which is headquartered in Chicago. The accuser could not get other women to back up her charges in the court of public opinion and has disappeared into the woodwork. No such accusations were levied against Herman during his time as president of Godfather's Pizza where he successfully brought the company out of bankruptcy, nor his time with Burger King where he returned a segment of Detroit Burger King franchises out of near bankruptcy to among the most profitable Burger Kings in the country. Herman has dropped back in the polls but still remains in the top three.

The next candidate to be elevated into the sunlight of the polls is Newt Gingrich. Under examination, he is found to be liberal in his approach to the "illegal immigrants" issue. He wants to make the residing illegal immigrants legal occupants in the United States while closing the border to further illegals. The only way I see this being acceptable is if they are denied the voting rights that Americans citizens are given.

I expect that if the main stream media can find something with which to denigrate Michelle Bachmann and Rick Santorum, they will bubble to the top of the polls for scrutiny against Romney. They have been shunned thus far.

Mitt Romney has not received the proctologic examination which has been given to the top Conservative candidates. Mitt is the 2012 John McCain. The nation's bane, The Affordable Care Act, AKA "Obamacare," is modeled after Massachusetts's near-bankrupt state healthcare system which Romney shoehorned in when he was governor of Massachusetts. Mitt is also a proponent of the scientifically debunked and ethically defamed global warming movement. These are two of the main platforms of today's progressive POTUS 44. Romney will be easy pickings for the progressives in 2012 if he is the chosen Republican candidate.

Assessing the damage to the Conservative candidates so far:

Rick Perry is known to be a seasoned politician with a liberal immigration view. Rick used an executive order to force the Vagisil immunization on all grade school girls in Texas.

Newt Gingrich is a strong Conservative until we look at his immigration view. He does not agree with the majority view that illegal immigrants are criminals in the United States and should be returned to their own country. The question remains whether or not he will abide by his oath to uphold the constitution and the laws enacted therein or dictate his plan to legitimize the illegals in the country by executive order.

Herman Cain faced an accusation of sexual abuse in the court of public opinion. The accusation was made by a woman who has a history of making similar accusations and losing her cases when her accusations were tried in court. Her case was settled out of court by the NRA for $35,000, and she agreed to leave the company. The settlement was finalized without including Herman in the decision.

Michelle Bachmann and Rick Santorum have not been scrutinized by the mainstream media yet.

It is obvious to me that the mainstream media is obfuscating the Conservatives' records and holding back Mitt Romney's weaknesses until the general election. A conservative Republican will beat POTUS 44, and the Democrats know this. If the Conservative voters succumb to the anxiety the mainstream media is trying to generate, they will elect another weak candidate, and the Republicans will lose another presidential election in the primaries by way of the same tactic the Democrats used in 2008.

Now let's take a deeper look at the standings:

Mitt Romney's poll rating has held steady at about 25 percent of the vote since February. That is approximately the percentage of Progressives and "wannabes." Ron Paul has his consistent 8 percent of the Libertarian voters. The remaining 67 percent are scattered among the rest of the Republican candidates with Cain and Gingrich in the top three. Even if Herman and Newt split the remainder of the Republican votes, they each beat Mitt by 12 percent. All you have to do is stand by your Conservative candidate. Don't give in to the anxiety the MSM is trying to generate. If the Conservative voters are not given clear choice in the general election, they will stay home as in 2008.

It is not my intention to boar you with repetition, but *this is the primaries. Vote for the candidate of your choice. Don't settle for a candidate that MSM tells you is the most electable. They want Conservatives to lose the presidential election. You* know *that!*

The primaries are more important than the general election. The current low turnout for the primary election gives the opposition a less daunting task to manipulate the opposition's election results as explained in the next segment. The voter has a clear choice in the general election. It could be the candidate your opposition party chose for you.

The Frustrations of the Registered Independent Voters

The number of registered Independent voters has been slowly increasing since the '50s. I assume this occurs because both the Democrat and Republican parties have been sliding left with each election. Most states, including Florida, have closed primaries. In a closed primary, the voters cast their vote for a candidate from the party in which the voter is registered. Republican voters choose from the field of Republican candidates. Democrat voters choose from the field of Democrat candidates, etc. The registered Independents just stand by and watch the primary election hoping for a good candidate in the general election.

Leading into the 2008 primaries, the Democrat National Committee put out a statement that John McCain was their choice for the Republican nominee for president. The Republicans had eight or ten candidates running in the primaries, and the primary voter turnout is historically low, presumably because most of the Republican voters don't know their candidates and leave the primary voting to those voters "in the know." Most of those voters don't research the candidates beyond what they hear and see on the mainstream media. John McCain won the Republican primary and was trounced in the general election. Voter turnout was sixty-nine million votes for Obama and sixty-one million votes for McCain.

Leading into the 2012 primaries, the mainstream media put out a statement that Mitt Romney was the only electable candidate in the Republican field. The Republicans had ten candidates running in the primaries. The voters obliged, and Romney won the Republican nomination for the presidential race. Mitt Romney was beat in the general election by POTUS 44. Voter turnout was sixty-one million votes for Obama and fifty-nine million votes for McCain.

Twelve million voters did not show up at the polls for the 2012 elections, nine million Democrat votes stayed home, and three million Republican votes did not show up in the 2012 general election. I don't want to be nitpicky, so I'll say the twelve million voters that didn't show up in the 2012 general election were mostly Independent voters and were frustrated with the candidates that came out of the primary. Those voters also did not participate in the primary where the presidential nominee is elected. The registered Independent voters disenfranchise themselves from the election process in most states.

The registered Independent voters can ease their discomfort by reregistering in the party of their choice up to thirty days prior to a primary, vote in the primary, and reregister again as Independent after the primary election. This way they can continue showing their indignation at the current political parties, if they insist, and still participate in the equally important election, the primary election.

Judging the Judges

In light of Obama's treatment of the Supreme Court of the United States at the 2010 State of the Union message, I find it hard to believe Justice Roberts is biased toward the Democrats and Obamacare. I think SCOTUS, in their two rulings this week, are holding the Democrats feet to the fire.

In the Arizona case, by dropping the three issues that mirror the federal government's primary responsibility and allowing the issue of state's verification of citizenship, they keep the current legislated superstructure in place, keep the spotlight on the Justice Department's refusal to perform its constitutional duty, and force the voters of this country to perform their constitutional duty by educating themselves on the issues and voting for the candidates that espouse the views that the voters hold dear.

The same applies to the ruling on Obamacare. H.R. 3200 was presented to our elected representatives and us voters with the title *America's Affordable Health Choices Act of 2009* with a heart of the *single payer mandate* to power the legislation and would not add to the taxpayers' burdens. The legislators were given three days to review the 2,700 pages of the legislation before they were expected to approve it. They approved it because they were told they "have to enact the bill before they can find out what is in it" by Nancy Pelosi and later admitted they did not read the bill. I must admit it has a cavalier sounding title, what can go wrong?

When the constitutionality of Obamacare was argued to the SCOTUS the single payer mandate was presented as a tax and the federal government has the constitutional authority to enact a tax on the citizens. The SCOTUS agrees with that definition and highlighted the fact that the single payer aspect of the bill is a tax. The five judges ruled in favor of Obamacare as constructionists. I don't like the outcome either. It makes me mad enough to go out and vote for something.

The conservative talk show hosts and bloggers are lambasting SCOTUS for not being Conservative activists in these two rulings. This progressive government is attributed with creating a nanny state by using activist liberal judges to back up their progressive legislation. Either activism creates a nanny state. Attempting to lay blame on the Supreme Court for supporting bad legislation deflects the audience's attention from the real problem which is uneducated voters. The voters are shirking their constitutional responsibility by voting without having backgrounds on the candidates they are selecting.

So where does the fault lay; with judge that interprets the law as it was constructed, with the politician that buys a pig-in-a-poke or votes for legislation because it has a cavalier sounding name, or the voter that re-elects that politician and expects different results from him the next time?

Do your research or find research sources you can trust. A candidate having a nice head of hair doesn't mean there are Conservative thought beneath the hair roots.

Compromise

So, let's look at a sample situation where compromise is demanded between Democrats (the left) and Republicans (the right) and let's make the Constitution of the United States an anchor point for the negotiations.

The Republicans state their position to be near where they want to be when the negotiations are finished. The Democrats include throwaways to surround their prize point in the negotiation. In negotiating both parties give up throwaways until the Democrats are stripped down to their prize point and dig in their heels. They scream "Look how much we've given in to you. You are not negotiating in good faith." The Republicans hang their head and say "Oh, alright. You have given up so much." And the Republicans take another step to the left and further away from the Constitution. Whether the Republicans are in the majority or the minority, conservatism loses every time in these negotiations.

This has been going on for so long that the Republican Party has been moved so far to the left, there is a huge void on the right, the Constitutional side of the equation. The Independents may not consider themselves Conservatives, but they are not happy with the direction America is being taken.

In the general elections of 2008 and 2012 the Republicans presented the voters the two most liberal candidates from the Republican primaries, McCain and Romney. Both were defeated by a Democrat candidate that has the thinnest resume and the worst intentions for our country and the capitalist system, the system that has made us the wealthiest and strongest country in history. I believe the Independents are totally discouraged from voting because they don't see a difference in the direction either party is taking this country.

7,598,898 that voted for the Democrat Presidential candidate in 2008 did not vote in 2012. I feel confident in assuming they didn't get the change they hoped. 1,343,280 that voted for the Republican Presidential candidate in 2008 did not vote in 2012. I feel confident assuming that the voters didn't see enough of a difference between the two parties' candidates to bother coming to the polls.

I think the RNC should stand up for the conservative Republican candidates when the opposition attacks them with lies and innuendos in the primaries. The RNC doesn't need to support a particular candidate. It needs to expose the lies that the left so freely use to besmirch the Conservative candidates they most fear.

A fellow incredulously once stated to me "Mitt Romney is a Mormon. How can you not see him as a Conservative"? I replied, "Nancy Pelosi Joe Biden and I are Catholics. I don't consider either of them to be Conservatives". Claiming a religious affiliation does not render all other political views of a candidate moot.

Over the years, the Progressives have tried to label Conservatives as "wingers," "wing nuts," "extreme right," "radical right," etc., etc., etc. The Republicans didn't defend themselves, they didn't express themselves in terms relative to the constitution. The Republican candidates are like piñatas, just quietly hanging there getting beat up until they break. The Progressives then walk away with the goods and leave the Republicans to pick up the trash.

A Final Election Observation

The next election is in 2016. As of this writing there are eight declared Republican candidates for the presidential race. The voters need to settle on only three or four candidates to consider in the primary.

If you haven't been paying attention, Duval County had two viable Republican candidates in the mayor race—Lenny Curry and Bill Bishop. Lenny Curry won out, and Lenny and Alvin Brown went on to the general election on May 19. Republican Bill Bishop publicly declared his support for Democrat Alvin Brown in the general election. Bill Bishop was a Democrat plant in the Republican field.

This same scenario played out in the Sheriff race. Jimmy Holderfield lost to Republican Mike Williams then publicly backed Democrat Ken Jefferson for sheriff in the general election.

Expect to see this same tactic applied to future political races in spades. If the Conservatives spread their votes out too thin, the progressive backed RINO in the race will surely win.

Cradle to Grave Single Payer Health Care

Progress is our most important product.

Free Prenatal Care—

Free sonograms to determine health and sex of your embryonic tissue.

Free abortion if you are not satisfied with the results of your free sonogram.

Free Child Care—

Free government childcare while you work and play. Your attentive government will raise your child to its specifications so you don't have to take time out of your busy life to wipe noses and bottoms.

Free children admission in the government-run CHIPS program. You know your healthy child's medical needs will be provided so you don't have to be bothered with the routine practitioner visits.

Free Education—

Rest assured your government will evaluate your child's educational needs and will assign your child to an appropriate study program based on your child's evaluation results. Rest assured the assigned study program will not tax your child's emotions and patience with harsh challenges.

Your child will not be pressured to advance beyond his predetermined abilities as determined by the standard evaluation results.

His monitor is sensitive to your child's needs and will react swiftly to protect your child's emotional wellbeing. Your child will be diverted to a temporary work camp if your child is determined to be exhausted from the rigors of the educational program. Of course your child will be granted the usual two diversions before being permanently assigned a productive and self-fulfilling lifelong career in a cheerful and structured work environment.

Free Health Care—

Throughout his government chosen career, your child will be provided the best healthcare that the government can provide a healthy, happy, and productive adult. Yes, your government wants to keep your child healthy, happy, and productive.

Free End of Life Care—

And of course, your child's productivity will wane at around age seventy. That is the standard retirement age. Along with productivity, your child's health will deteriorate. Don't fret. It's in good hands. Government health insurance will be your child's for the rest of its life or until age seventy-five, whichever comes first. Imagine going for a walk in your neighborhood park whenever you want, going for a ride with your favorite life partner or significant other on a bike, a tandem bike, of course. You feel so good about conserving energy and saving the planet.

After age seventy, your retired child will automatically be entered into the caring pre-hospice program where he will meet with his assigned caring doctor to discuss end of life planning. This free program will introduce your child to homeopathic self-medication, and the child will learn to increasingly rely on self-medication. At age seventy-five, he will be fully trained and reliant on self-medication for most common ills. For the few other serious ills, your child will automatically be enrolled in the updated gentle and caring hospice program.

Wish you wellness and good health,

Your caring government

You Need to Pass the Bill to Find Out What's in It

You may need to reread the chapter on education to see how far the United States education system has declined. The progressives felt the Americans have been dummied down enough to swallow this logic, and they were right. Obamacare was passed in 2010.

One of the architects was Jonathan Gruber, a Massachusetts Institute of Technology professor, credited the passing of the Affordable Care Act to the stupidity of the average American.[21]

We Dodged a Bullet

Medicare funding is 100 percent federal government responsibility and paid out from a portion of the Federal Insurance Contributions Act (FICA) taxes collected from taxpayers. Medicaid management is the responsibility of each state government, and the funding is shared with the federal government with 45 percent of the responsibility being the state share and 55 percent is paid by the federal government.

When POTUS 44 presented the Affordable Care Act (ACA/Obamacare) of 2010, he modeled it after Medicaid—all the while he was in the process of bankrupting America. If he succeeded in destroying the American economy, the states would be stuck with 100 percent of their Medicaid bill and that would bankrupt the states within a year. This is a very devious plan. Fortunately, the United States economy is more resilient then POTUS 44 thought.

Immigration

Marco Rubio and Paul Ryan are the two prominent figures of a "gang of eight" of 2013 that successfully spearheaded an amnesty bill for illegal immigrants through the Senate. It doesn't even pretend to be stronger than the amnesty of 1986 which left the borders open.

---

[21] Chumley, 2014

Marco Rubio presented himself as a solid Conservative who would uphold the US Constitution and never grant amnesty to the illegals when he successfully ran for the Senate in 2010. Paul Ryan was Mitt Romney's running mate in the 2012 presidential elections. The Romney/Ryan team was the last hope of the Republicans who want to take this country back from the Socialists. Both men have greatly disappointed the conservative American voters.

The illegal immigrants became criminals the moment they set foot on United States soil without the knowledge and consent of the American government. The proposed amnesty legislation of 2013 denigrates the US Constitution by overlooking the federal government's responsibility to secure our country's borders. An implementation of this proposed amnesty legislation kicks the American-born citizen to the curb. It mocks the legal immigrants who arrived in the United States with government papers in hand, learned English, studied the Daughters of the American Revolution Citizenship Manual, passed the citizenship test, and expressed their allegiance to the United States when taking the oath of citizenship.

These illegal immigrants are already being given welfare benefits that are not easily given to American citizens and legal immigrants, and the total welfare benefits given to an illegal immigrant exceed the household income of most of the low-income American families.

How Patriotism Is Convoluted into Racism

Today is September 2011. One of the few constitutional functions of the United States government is to protect the country's borders. Mexicans are flying the American flag upside down and below the Mexican flag on school flag poles in California. Mexicans and OTMs (other than Mexican) are wading onto the United States from Mexico between checkpoints, many carrying drugs and guns. Border patrol agents, farmers, and even vacationers are being killed by these lawbreakers along our southern border and in our southern cities. Our attorney general Eric Holder tells our ATF agents to stand down when asked for permission to intercept shipments of weapons illegally being taken across the border into Mexico. The Tea Party stands in opposition to the illegal immigrants running around freely in the US. The Tea Party is labeled "racist" for its opposition to illegal immigration.

The terms *racist* and *racism* have been used successfully to silence opposition to activities by the progressive movement and is intended to upend American social and religious morals. The terms *racist* and *racism* were reintroduced by the Progressives by resurrecting the concept of slavery which had been legislated out of existence in the United States over a hundred years ago, and they built on that. The movement has been successful so far because our civil skin, the genteel American, had been taking the abrasions without a whimper. The subdermal layer, the moderate and progressive politicians, have no backbone and in many cases have sided with the illegal immigrants against the constitution of the United States ignoring their oath of office to protect "the Constitution." We are now down to the meat and backbone of the country, the job producers and workers of the country, being labeled racist for siding against illegal immigration and insisting the United States government do its job and protect the United States borders and legal residents. We have taken notice and reject the labels.

Finally, in labeling the Tea Party as racists in these times, the Progressives are attempting to bring the black Americans into the same group as illegal immigrants. The NAACP has joined the progressives in labeling the Tea Party as racist. The black Americans should be taking serious umbrage with this manipulation and take their progressive leaders to task for disenfranchising them from their American heritage and including them with the illegal immigrant criminals.

Tea Party Is Dead?

As I see it, the Tea Parties as originally created have evolved or died out. The 2010 elections was the apex for the Tea Party movement. The excitement was fed by the spontaneity of the corner sign waving and public display of support for each other for a common cause. While this was going on, the political insiders of the Tea Party picked up on the undercurrents below the surface of the political process and diverted their attention to addressing these issues. *You might be looking out at the Atlantic Ocean and see calmly undulating waves presenting a serene scene. You look beneath the surface, and you see the carnivorous activity of the predators feeding on the smaller fish on down the food chain.* The street corners were abandoned for more important issues, so the public display disappeared leaving the Progressives to assume the Tea Party movement was dead. The Tea Party movement is not visible on the surface as when it first started, but the movement lives on and grows in the Conservatives.

Up pops the next generation of patriotic organizations like Breitbart News and many remaining tea party groups around the country. The challenge for them is to keep the attention of future generations on the politicians they elect and on preserving the Constitution of the United States. I wonder if we can set up a website that will broadcast our politician's vote on a pertinent issue for instance. Possibly have real-time reporting. We've seen that Facebook and Twitter are filtered by Liberals and won't allow such content. The young are glued to their mobile phones. They don't read the newspapers. Their attention span is diminished. They are acclimated to short bursts of information. We can change the trend by restoring our education system back to the structure it was operating under in 1965. Each state controlled its own curriculum and its own education standards.

On Unions

Unions will intimidate employees in an open election. I was a union employee for a while in my youth. In the union environment, the "masses" ride on the coattails of a few producers. I've watched a union take down the world-renowned bridge and structural company, American Bridge Company, with its demands in the late 1960s. You can see the same scenario acting out in today's auto industry. Unions were needed at the outset. After an equilibrium was reached between union and management, the unions started overreaching to justify their existence. This overreach is what has closed companies' doors and turned hard-working people against the unions.

Thoughts on Political Correctness

I first heard the term *political correctness* in the mid nineteen-seventies. When a fellow explained how it works, I said, "That is the biggest conversation killer I've heard of." As it has developed over the years, political correctness is a pry bar that is being used to tear America and our society apart. Political correctness is used to stifle thoughts, actions, and constructive conversations, and nobody has come up with a way to remove or counter this pry bar. It has been very frustrating for me.

Americans have suffered setbacks in their freedoms and wealth since political correctness proponents were allowed to stifle and then trample the US Constitution.

Political correctness's definition and use is morphed into whatever serves the progressives' needs at the moment.

I want to introduce a new phrase into our lexicon: "constitutional correctness." The Constitution is well defined, and most of the American people are aware of it. Constitutional correctness trumps political correctness whenever the two are in opposition. This will encourage us to become better versed in the Constitution, the Bill of Rights, and the Federalist papers.

The United States Constitution has been around for over 225 years. It defines the base for the laws of our Democratic republic.

Under the United States Constitution, the United States has grown to be the most powerful, wealthiest, most technologically advanced, and most benevolent country this world has ever seen.

America's poor are better off than 68 percent of the world's population.[22] Historically, the lifespan of a republic has been two hundred to two hundred and twenty-five years. Our United States of America has existed for 244 years and appears to be on its last legs. The Constitution of the United States defines the framework that

---

[22] Worstall, 2013

holds the union together, and the second amendment is the backbone of this constitution.

> About the time our original thirteen states adopted their new constitution in 1787, Alexander Tyler, a Scottish history professor at the University of Edinburgh, had this to say about the fall of the Athenian Republic some 2,000 years earlier:
>
> "A democracy is always temporary in nature; it simply cannot exist as a permanent form of government."
>
> "A democracy will continue to exist up until the time that voters discover they can vote themselves generous gifts from the public treasury."
>
> "From that moment on, the majority always vote for the candidates who promise the most benefits from the public treasury, with the result that every democracy will finally collapse due to loose fiscal policy, which is always followed by a dictatorship."
>
> "The average age of the world's greatest republics from the beginning of history, has been about 200 years."
>
> "During those 200 years, those nations always progressed through the following sequence:
>
> 1. from bondage to spiritual faith;
> 2. from spiritual faith to great courage;
> 3. from courage to liberty;
> 4. from liberty to abundance;
> 5. from abundance to complacency;
> 6. from complacency to apathy;
> 7. from apathy to dependence;
> 8. from dependence back into bondage.

So WHERE are we, citizens of the United States, in the historically proven Life Cycle of Nations?" (Source: http://www.freerepublic.com/focus/f-chat...; http://commonsensegovernment.com/the-tytler-cycle-revisited/)

America is about thirty percent into stage 7. The complacency stage in stage 5 is the beginning of the deterioration of America.

The Silent Language of Deception

Taqiyya. It is Allah-approved deception against non-Muslims.

In Islam, you're allowed to lie (sin!) against a non-Muslim without fear of punishment. Once a non-Muslim converts, the table changes and the person can't be lied to anymore and this individual wakes up to the hard reality of Islam with the added caveat that apostasy is likely to relieve him or her from their burdened head.[23]

Taqiyya has been practiced by the progressive politicians since they began taking over the Democrat party in 1969. The American voters have been lamenting the fact that once the politician takes office he appears to have forgotten the promises he made during his campaign for the office. This was most notable in the aftermath of the 2008 presidential election. Do you remember these statements?

"If you like your doctor, you can keep your doctor."

"Your household insurance premiums will be reduced by twenty-five hundred dollars per year."

Through the years, there are many examples of campaign promises being forgotten while the votes are still being counted. The same campaign promises come around every election. That has changed with the election of POTUS 45 in spite of the attempts by the deep state government's attempts to block everything he attempted to accomplish. POTUS 45 is slowed down but remains undaunted in fulfilling his campaign promises. He finds a way. How refreshing!

---

[23] Thereligionofpeace.com, 2019

Interrogations Benefitted the United
States and the World

When you can't see the forest for the trees, you need to step
back and take in the big picture.

World War I was a global war centered in Europe that began
on July 28, 1914 and lasted until November 11, 1918. *More than
nine million combatants and seven million civilians died as a result of
the war,* a casualty rate exacerbated by the belligerents' technologi-
cal and industrial sophistication and tactical stalemate. It was one of
the deadliest conflicts in history, paving the way for major political
changes, including revolutions in many of the nations involved. The
United States joined the Allies in 1917.

World War II was a global war that lasted from 1939 to 1945,
though related conflicts began earlier. It involved the vast majority of
the world's nations—including all of the great powers—eventually
forming two opposing military alliances, the Allies and the Axis. It
was the most widespread war in history and directly involved more
than a hundred million people from over thirty countries. In a state
of "total war," the major participants threw their entire economic,
industrial, and scientific capabilities behind the war effort, erasing
the distinction between civilian and military resources. *Marked by
mass deaths of civilians, including the Holocaust (during which approximately eleven million people were killed) and the strategic bombing of
industrial and population centers (during which approximately one million people were killed, including the use of two nuclear weapons in
combat), it resulted in an estimated fifty million to eighty-five million
fatalities.* These made World War II the deadliest conflict in human
history. The United States joined the allies in 1942 after recovering
from Japanese attack on the naval facility at Pearl Harbor in Hawaii.[24]

---

[24] En.wikipedia.org, 2019

The Korean war started in June of 1950 and ended In July 1953. In all, *some five million soldiers and civilians lost their lives* during the war.[25]

In Vietnam, direct US military involvement ended on August 15, 1973 as a result of the Case-Church Amendment passed by the US Congress. The capture of Saigon by the North Vietnamese Army in April 1975 marked the end of the war, and North and South Vietnam were reunified the following year. The war exacted a huge human cost in terms of fatalities (see Vietnam War casualties). *Estimates of the number of Vietnamese service members and civilians killed vary from 800,000 to 3.1 million. Some 200,000 to 300,000 Cambodians, 20,000 to 200,000 Laotians, and 58,220 US service members also died in the conflict.*

Iraq war, approximately *500,000* deaths in Iraq as direct or indirect result of the war from March 2003 to June 2011 (Source: http://en.wikipedia.org/wiki/Casualties_of_the_Iraq_War),

The Iraq War introduced the use of drones and precision-guided missiles, and the civilian and military casualties were reduced greatly compared to previous wars. The precise execution of these weapons are not possible without intelligence from covert ground resources gathering the information necessary to aim these precise weapons. This covert information is collected by operations such as the CIA orchestrates.

The Democrats of today are unable to garner the sympathy of the citizens to stop the military operations by advertising body counts (which they stopped when POTUS 44 took office) and are now publishing CIA interrogation secrets. With such information leaks by the Democrats and the media, who will stand with the United States in times of conflict. I heard one military man state that it is aiding and abetting the enemy which falls under the definition of treason.

If our covert operations are disassembled, future wars will have to revert back to carpet bombing and nuclear threats endangering millions of military and civilian lives.

---

[25] History.com, 2019

The Citizen Legislator

Today we have career politicians. Many of these politicians have never worked in the private sector. I see no problem in term limits. The separate and unequal retirement benefits for legislators need to be done away with. Once the politicians have completed their elected terms, they need to go back home and live under the laws they have legislated for the voters. They need to retire under the same rules they have enacted for the voters.

"Put It in God's Hands"

God gave me the talents to fulfill my purpose on Earth. God did not give me a purpose for which I am not equipped. My primary talent is the ability to learn "new (to me)" ideas and to understand "new (to me)" approaches. Each of us have our own envelope, and each of our envelopes can expand at different rates and have different limits.

If I get myself in a situation that I don't understand and don't want to learn how to work with it, I will not "put it in God's hands." He doesn't want it. Why would God want to be bothered with solving a worldly problem? It won't do him any good. I am in this situation through my own actions, and God gave me the talent work my way through it. It may take a different approach, or I may have to study it more. If I still can't handle it, I may have maxed out my envelope and should just drop it and go on to something else. "Putting it in God's hands" isn't going to make me a better person, and the notion certainly isn't going to interest God. I still attend church services on a regular schedule.

Amen. Hallelujah.

The Tea Party Is Dead?

As I see it, the tea parties as originally created have evolved or died out. The 2010 elections was the apex for the Tea Party movement. The excitement was fed by the spontaneity of the corner sign waving and public display of support for each other for a common cause. While this was going on, the political insiders picked up on the undercurrents below the surface of the political process and diverted their attention to addressing these issues. *You might be looking out at the Atlantic Ocean and see calmly undulating waves presenting a serene scene. You look beneath the surface, and you see the carnivorous activity of the predators feeding on the smaller fish on down the food chain.* The street corners were abandoned for more important issues, so the public display disappeared leaving the press to assume the Tea Party movement was dead.

Up pops the next generation of patriots like Oath Keepers. The challenge for them is to keep the attention of future generations on the politicians they elect and on preserving the Constitution of the United States. I wonder if we can set up an email file that will broadcast our politician's vote on a pertinent issue for instance. Possibly have real-time reporting. We've seen that Facebook and Twitter are filtered by Liberals. The young are glued to their mobile phones. They don't read the newspapers. Their attention span is diminished. They are acclimated to short bursts of information. We can't change that until we change our education system back to where it was in 1965.

The Tea Party Is Not Dead

The Tea Party has led to the exposure of ACORN's illegal activities in all aspects of American life. ACORN and much, much more lies beneath the surface. The direction the waves travel is dependent on the direction of the wind and is superficial and temporary. The forces that control the atmosphere globally lie beneath the surface. Keep your focus on the waves, and you won't see much of the Tea Party.

Rebirth or Abortion

I haven't been watching much television in the last couple of years. I lost interest when I discovered the internet gave me a better feel for what is really going on than listening to CNN and the others. CNN really took off with its coverage of the first Gulf War. It was a major blow to my confidence in television journalism when I compared the RNC coverage by CNN (lack of coverage) and C-SPAN (live coverage) in the 2000 election. CNN had a slow-talking announcer asking dull trivia questions about previous RNC events against slow background music. I became tired of it in a hurry and switched to C-SPAN for RNC coverage. What a difference. There were dynamic speakers addressing cheering delegates. Everybody was having a good time except those people watching CNN.

I am starting to save my pennies for a HAM radio in case the current progressive government succeeds in controlling the internet content. Our overseas friends are keenly interested in what happens here. The United States is the shining light on the hill in their eyes. *They could see that there was a political system that worked. Its failure today is not a failure of the system but a failure of the citizens to care for their political system.*

The United States have gone through a republic's life cycle—birth in the Revolutionary War, Declaration of Independence at great cost to most of the signers, building of a capitalist nation based on individual freedom and personal responsibility and resolved a major internal conflict with the Civil War. Despite wanting to mind its own business, the United States was blindsided with the attack on Pearl Harbor while the world's attention was focused on Europe's war. The

United States recovered and mobilized to defeat the offensive force in Europe and Japan. The United States then did what no other victor nation has ever done in civilization's history. After defeating the morally and politically corrupt leaders of those countries, the United States helped the citizens of the offending nations rebuild their countries. We (I was born at the end of the war and immigrated to the United States) explored space and the depths of our oceans, all while fighting several other wars on foreign soil. All this in 225 years. After these accomplishments, we started showing our age.

We became occupied with our own wellbeing and ignored the signs of aging of our nation. We hosted barbecues for our golfing buddies, discussing the last round, and paid no attention to the direction our country was being taken by our elected leaders. *But we elected them, and we are responsible for their actions.*

Today, we are in a fight for the survival of our country. Will we let it die at the mountain top, or will we help it be born again while on the mountain top? *Will we fight for the rebirth of our nation or sit on our hands and witness the abortion of this nation? I choose to fight.*

True the Vote, Get Out the Vote, then What?

We have two major projects working toward the 2012 elections, "True the Vote" to prepare a voting stage for a fair election and "Get Out the Vote" to bring the Conservative voters out to the polls. It seems to me we need one more leg to give this platform stability. Once we get the voters reinvigorated, I can only envision a box of springs being dumped onto the floor when the voters get to the voting booth. I don't know where they will end up.

I propose we add websites such as http://conservativevoterresearch.webs.com/ (the "original" Conservative citizen) as the third leg to give the voters direction. Many have given up saying, "It doesn't matter who I vote for, they are all the same" or "They all conjure up the same promising images before they get the vote and then go back to their old ways after the election." This research site is intended as a resource for the voter that does not have the time, the inclination or the resources to research the viable candidates that qualify for the

2012 elections. I estimate this covers about 80 percent of the voters. The remaining 20 percent will do their own research and that is good. The only problem is their research is limited to the higher levels of government. They ignore the primordial stew where their chosen candidates were indoctrinated in the government roles at the local level. Unfortunately this candidate research site only covers Northeast Florida.

A New Revolutionary War

In the 2012 presidential primary, Mitt Romney's campaign followed the historical Republican strategy of presenting him as a moderate for the primary and attempted to come across as a Conservative for the general election.

With the advent of the Tea Party, this strategy is failing. The Conservative voters' memories are getting longer. One indication is that thirteen million voters did not show up for the 2012 election that voted in 2008. My analysis tells me the thirteen million voters didn't see enough of a difference between their choices to be bothered to show up at the polls. Another indication is that, in the 2016 election, the three front runners have no political history. They reflect the makeup of our founding fathers. We are having another Revolutionary War, this one between capitalism and communism with Donald Trump being our generation's George Washington. I am not aware of any person that would be able to take the innuendoes and lies targeting President Trump all the while he is able to work around the obstacles Democrat Socialists keep throwing at him and fulfill his campaign promises.

I differentiate myself from the analysts that appear on television. They present "in-depth" analysis of election results and predictions using statistics, charts, and psychological diagnostics. Their observations don't jibe with the events on the street. Today's voters aren't reflected in the models that the campaigns have developed over the decades. The Conservative voters are organized in tea parties across the country and have learned from the 2008 and 2012 elections that the media, the polls, and the party leaders are not to be trusted. The Conservatives are, for the most part, ignoring them.

The party leaders are still relying on the "tried and true" strategies of the past. Today, the adage of the '90s, "Inquiring minds want to know," is more in play that ever before in politics.

> "*One of the penalties for refusing to participate in politics, is that you end up being governed by your inferiors*" (Plato).

We Have A Conservative Congress
Now What?

Over the past forty years, the Republicans had political control over the country many times and lost it. From my own experience, I believe we Republicans lost it because we brush the dust off our hands smugly saying, "That'll teach them" and turn our backs to resume our politically disinterested lives. The DC machine then takes these freshmen and indoctrinates them into the longstanding political ways. We need to change the longstanding political ways in DC. To do this, we need to stay just as engaged in the political process after the election as we were before the election, otherwise all the changes the Tea Party helped introduce into DC will be undone by year end. We must not turn our backs on them again.

What's Happening?

The United States is a Democratic Republic. History has documented that the life span of a Republic is 200 to 225 years. The Democratic Republic of the United States of America is 244 years old. Forty percent of the population is on welfare, the president of the United States is an *AINO* who despises this country and is working to collapse it. He has weakened the military, strangled the economy, pushed away the allies of America, and has nursed his JV team (ISIS) into a full-fledged fighting force that is taking on entire countries.

The walls of this Republic are crumbling. Since 1992, democracy has pushed this republic down the slippery slope toward socialism. In 2008, the voters chose a president that increased the welfare benefits and opened the borders welcoming in any foreigners to grab what benefits they could get and vote for the guy that gave the benefits to them. This outcome was cultivated by the Democrat party and sanctioned by the establishment Republican party.

Runaway Automobile
Runaway Government

There is an automobile whose gas pedal is stuck to the floor so the driver can't slow it down by taking his foot off of the pedal. The brake line has a leak and the harder the driver presses on the brake pedal, the faster the brake fluid leaks out and he can't stop the vehicle using the method that was designed into the automobile to stop it under normal circumstances. The cable for the emergency brake is rusted through due to lack of attention, and pulling the emergency brake doesn't work as it was designed. The steering assembly has been damaged, and the steering wheel is disengaged from the wheels. The automobile is off the road, and the driver knows there is a cliff ahead, somewhere.

The panicked driver might open the door and drag his foot to try and stop the auto before it goes over the cliff. The panicked driver might jump out of the automobile and let it destroy itself and the other screaming passengers in the vehicle. Neither scenario has a happy ending.

The logical driver would turn the ignition key to off. The vehicle would coast to a stop, and the damaged vehicle would await repairs to the major control features to restore the vehicle to its original design specifications. In this scenario, the damaged vehicle is repaired, the passengers are safe. Though the trip is delayed, it can be continued safely.

There is a government whose president is inexperienced and is in the driver's seat of his country and is taking the country toward a cliff. He has the pedal to the metal and ignores the screaming citizens' pleas to stop the mad rush forward. By design, it is up to the other two branches of the government and the citizens to bring the government to a stop and wait for repairs before the country is damaged beyond repair.

It is in the best interest of the United States to slow or, better yet, stop this government's advance in the current direction. The House of Representatives have failed our Republic. It is up to the Republican Senate to shut the country down before it is destroyed.

Washington, DC politicians were becoming known as a runaway government. In 1980, the American voters elected Ronald Reagan as president. President Reagan exercised the leadership America was looking for. He strengthened the military, improved the economic environment to nourish American productivity, and was responsible for Russia taking down the iron curtain dividing East and West Berlin Germany and ending the cold war.

Today, the United States is in worse shape than before President Reagan's election. By applying deductive reasoning, if you fix a problem and it recurs, then you applied a fix to a symptom and not the problem.

"*All you capitalists that want to show up to Lake Michigan, I'm going to start organizing,*" he screamed from the Chicago Mercantile Exchange on February 19, 2009. It was time, Santelli said, for another Tea Party.

Tea Parties started popping up in communities all across the country. These Tea Parties are not political parties and their membership consists of Conservative taxpayers wanting to regain control of their government. The Tea Party influence was already apparent in the 2010 elections where Republicans regained control of the chamber they had lost in the 2006 midterm elections, picking up a net total of sixty-three seats and erasing the gains Democrats made in 2006 and 2008.

In 2012, nine million Democrats and three million Republican voters who voted in 2008 general election did not cast ballots. Obama won re-election by two million votes. There was stunned silence across the country for five months, a period of *Post-Election Stress Disorder*. I happened upon two of the absent Republican voters in the first two years since the 2012 election, and in the brief conversation I had with them, both said, "Never again am I going to miss an election." It appears to me that a second Revolutionary War has begun in these United States. With the Constitution and its amendments backing the revolutionaries, there was no need for armed insurrection yet.

In the 2014 House elections, Republicans won sixteen seats from Democrats, while three Republican-held seats turned Democratic. Combined with the Republican gains made in 2010, the total number of Democratic-held House seats lost under POTUS 44's presidency in midterm elections rose to seventy-seven with these elections. Republicans took nine Senate seats from the Democrats.

It is no surprise to me that, from the outset of the 2016 presidential coverage, three of the four top contenders have no political experience on their resume. The fourth is an outsider and is openly despised by both political parties on the hill. The more nuances and outright lies the media puts out about each of these candidates the more each rises in the polls. It appears the sleeping Conservative giant has been awakened and is alert. The political experiment of 1776 has run its course. When this revolution calms, the country will not be the same as in the last 244 years.

The Democratic Republic of the United States of America has fostered the most successful society this world has ever seen. But as a Republic, it has run its course.

The Democratic Republic of the United States of America 2.0

You've heard many times that doing the same thing over again with the expectation of different results is the definition of insanity.

I repeat: *"If you fix a problem and it recurs, then you applied a fix to a symptom and not the problem." Runaway government is the symptom. The problem is runaway democracy.*

When the polls open on Election Day, every citizen over the age of 18 will be able to cast a vote. It is a privilege we take for granted, one that defines our nation as a democracy. But universal suffrage—letting everyone vote—did not appear overnight with the ratification of our Constitution. Two hundred years ago, you had to be white, male, and wealthy in order to vote. The three people profiled below dedicated their lives to changing that fact. Without them, suffrage might still be the privilege of a defined few. In order to cast a vote in the new democracy, one had to be white (except in a few Northern states), male (except in New Jersey, where women voted until 1807), and a landowner (nearly everywhere).

August 26, 1920, after two-thirds of the states had ratified the 19th Amendment to the Constitution, women won the right to vote.

That summer, with northern Liberals up in arms over news of southern racism, President Lyndon B. Johnson signs the Voting Rights Act, guaranteeing African-Americans the right to vote during the height of the American Civil Rights Movement *on August 6, 1965, and Congress later amended the Act five times to expand its protections. Section 2 is a general provision that prohibits every state and local gov-*

ernment from imposing any voting law that results in discrimination against racial or language minorities. Other general provisions specifically outlaw literacy tests and similar devices that were historically used to disenfranchise racial minorities. These devices help distinguish between knowledgeable and ignorant voters. The ignorant voters have to rely on and are influenced by a knowledgeable voter and merely parrot the knowledgeable voter's choice multiplying his vote by the magnitude of his sphere of influence. This defeats the intent of one man, one vote guaranteed by the constitution.

In 1993 President Clinton signed the "Motor Voter Act" into law. This opened the gates for anyone who applies for a driver license to register to vote. The act stated that the voter registration applicant must be a US citizen but blocked the supervisors of election from verifying the citizenship status of the applicant. They have to accept the word of the applicant. This voting act was the Segway to lawsuits prohibiting supervisors of elections from removing ineligible voters from their voter database.

To reign in runaway democracy, I propose a constitutional amendment that voting right be suspended from any citizen whose income consists of 75 percent or more of welfare for more than six consecutive months. The voting right will be restored after one year of tax paying status and application for restoration of voting rights with the local supervisor of elections who will verify the application.

To keep the voters active in their government between elections, I propose a constitutional amendment that allows for the recall of any elected or appointed federal employee by approval of 60 percent of the voters in the House of Representatives. The recall would be initiated by popular vote of 10 percent of the legal registered voters in the area affected. Elected and appointed officials do occasionally abuse their positions and need to be removed as soon as possible.

Reverting back to "The walls of this Republic are crumbling" and the introduction of the Tea Party to the American political scene, I see three possible outcomes of this revolution when the dust settles:

The Tea Party Conservatives succeed in restoring fiscal, social, and political conservatism in the Democratic Republic of the United States 2.0. The original constitution of the United States will remain with a few more amendments to reign in runaway democracy, limit the scope of executive orders, and stop government overreach. It would be wise to provide for recall elections for the Supreme Court members. A radical POTUS 44 only recognizes the religion of Islam, which does not exist without Sharia law. Sharia law is incompatible with the United States constitution; therefore, radical Muslims cannot exist in the United States and must be deported. When the historians have documented this period, these rebellious taxpayers will be known as patriots.

The second likely outcome is the Tea Party fails, and Communism takes over these United States. The Tea Party members are labeled hoodlums, and the leaders are jailed. The radical Muslim population continues to increase, and the LGBTQ population is shunned as in Russia.

The third likely outcome is the radical Muslims overrun the United States. The American infidels are called on to convert to Islam or be enslaved or beheaded. The LGBTQ population will also be beheaded or thrown off of tall buildings or worse.

The LGBTQ members are known to the government with the registration of same-sex marriages, various ways of identifying same-sex relationships, and identifying that part of the population that is woefully uneducated in general biology.

Bibliography

Militaryfactory.com. (2019). *American War Deaths Throughout History*. [online] Available at: https://www.militaryfactory.com/american_war_deaths.asp [Accessed 26 Oct. 2019].

Miller, P. (2019). *A Bio. of America: The Rise of Capitalism—Transcript*. [online] Learner.org. Available at: https://www.learner.org/series/biographyofamerica/prog07/transcript/page02.html [Accessed 27 Oct. 2019].

Alinsky, S. (2019). *Rules for Radicles*. [online] http://www.crossroad.to. Available at: http://www.crossroad.to/Quotes/communism/alinsky.html [Accessed 27 Oct. 2019].

Irvine, S. and Nitzberg, A. (2019). *The Origins of Political Correctness*. [online] Accuracy In Academia. Available at: https://www.academia.org/the-origins-of-political-correctness/ [Accessed 27 Oct. 2019].

Courtois, S., Werth, N., Penne, J., Paczkowski, A., Bartosek, K. and Margolin, J. (1999). *The Black Book of Communism*. [online] En.wikipedia.org. Available at: https://en.wikipedia.org/wiki/The_Black_Book_of_Communism [Accessed 27 Oct. 2019].

Walters, J. (2013). *Communism Killed 94M in 20th Century, Feels Need to Kill Again.* [online] Reason.com. Available at: https://reason.com/2013/03/13/communism-killed-94m-in-20th-century/ [Accessed 27 Oct. 2019].

En.wikipedia.org. (2019). *Mass killings under communist regimes.* [online] Available at: https://en.wikipedia.org/wiki/Mass_killings_under_communist_regimes [Accessed 27 Oct. 2019].

En.wikipedia.org. (2013). *The Communist Manifesto.* [online] Available at: https://en.wikipedia.org/wiki/The_Communist_Manifesto [Accessed 28 Oct. 2019].

Cs.stanford.edu. (2019). *Communism: In China.* [online] Available at: https://cs.stanford.edu/people/eroberts/cs201/projects/communism-computing-china/china.html [Accessed 28 Oct. 2019].

En.wikipedia.org. (2019). *We will bury you.* [online] Available at: https://en.wikipedia.org/wiki/We_will_bury_you [Accessed 28 Oct. 2019].

WikiDiff. (2019). *Progressivism vs Socialism—What's the difference?.* [online] Available at: https://wikidiff.com/progressivism/socialism [Accessed 28 Oct. 2019].

Investmentoffice.com. (2019). *2. Birth Rate Needed to Maintain Current Population.* [online] Available at: https://www.investmentoffice.com/io/Investment_Thoughts/Beyond_Finance/2_Birth_Rate_Needed_to_Maintain_Current_Population.php [Accessed 28 Oct. 2019].

Kangor, P. (2012). *The Nation's Top "Progressives"…and Socialists and Communists.* [online] The Institute for Faith and Freedom. Available at: https://www.faithandfreedom.com/the-nations-top-progressives-and-socialists-and-communists/ [Accessed 28 Oct. 2019].

HistoryNet. (2019). *World War II.* [online] Available at: https://www.historynet.com/world-war-ii [Accessed 28 Oct. 2019].

Alinsky, S. (1971). *Saul Alinsky's Rules for Radicals.* [online] Crossroad. to. Available at: http://www.crossroad.to/Quotes/communism/alinsky.htm [Accessed 29 Oct. 2019].

Adams, J. (2014). *A Primer on "Motor Voter": Corrupted Voter Rolls and the Justice Department's Selective Failure to Enforce Federal Mandates.* [online] The Heritage Foundation. Available at: https://www.heritage.org/election-integrity/report/primer-motor-voter-corrupted-voter-rolls-and-the-justice-departments [Accessed 29 Oct. 2019].

En.wikipedia.org. (2019). *1968 Democratic National Convention.* [online] Available at: https://en.wikipedia.org/wiki/1968_Democratic_National_Convention [Accessed 29 Oct. 2019].

En.wikipedia.org. (2019). *Antifa (United States).* [online] Available at: https://en.wikipedia.org/wiki/Antifa_(United_States) [Accessed 29 Oct. 2019].

Crossroad.to. (1971). *Saul Alinsky's Rules for Radicals.* [online] Available at: http://www.crossroad.to/Quotes/communism/alinsky.htm [Accessed 29 Oct. 2019].

Allgov.com. (2019). *AllGov—Departments*. [online] Available at: http://www.allgov.com/departments/department-of-education?detailsDepartmentID=584#controversiescont [Accessed 29 Oct. 2019].

Chumley, C. (2014). *Obamacare architect: We passed law due to 'stupidity of the American voter'*. [online] The Washington Times. Available at: https://www.washingtontimes.com/news/2014/nov/10/obamacare-architect-we-passed-law-due-to-stupidity/ [Accessed 29 Oct. 2019].

Worstall, T. (2013). *Astonishing Numbers: America's Poor Still Live Better Than Most Of The Rest Of Humanity*. [online] Forbes.com. Available at: https://www.forbes.com/sites/timworstall/2013/06/01/astonishing-numbers-americas-poor-still-live-better-than-most-of-the-rest-of-humanity/#178c2d1c54ef [Accessed 29 Oct. 2019].

Thereligionofpeace.com. (2019). *Taqiyya: Deception and Lying in Islam*. [online] Available at: https://www.thereligionofpeace.com/pages/quran/taqiyya.aspx [Accessed 29 Oct. 2019].

En.wikipedia.org. (2019). *World War II*. [online] Available at: https://en.wikipedia.org/wiki/World_War_II [Accessed 29 Oct. 2019].

History.com. (2019). *Korean War*. [online] Available at: https://www.history.com/topics/korea/korean-war [Accessed 29 Oct. 2019].

About the Author

John Sauer was born on the way out of Kaisersteinbruch, Austria, a Russian concentration camp, after the American army opened the gates of the camp at the end of the war and told the Russian captives to go home. The family home was in the Croatian part of Yugoslavia, but the home had been taken over. This was a Communist country. The family immigrated to the United States in 1949 and eventually settled in Gary, Indiana in 1951.

John attended Catholic schools through high school and received a degree in computer programming from Purdue University Calumet Campus. His career spanned forty years working on developing and maintaining business applications on large IBM equipment.

After retiring, John and his wife of thirty years moved to Texas for a few years. While he was there, the Tea Party movement was started, and he went to an occupied street corner to see what was going on. After talking with a few attendees and observing what was going on, he signed up. He acquired an interest in candidate research. He didn't take long to realize how poorly his previous approach to voting was. When he moved to Florida, he continued his candidate research on the first coast.